Trust

By

Dottie Randazzo

Trust

by

Dottie Randazzo

Published by:

Creative Dreaming

6433 Topanga Cyn. Blvd.

Woodland Hills, CA 91303

ISBN 978-0-6151-7664-2

By Dottie Randazzo

Praying 101 for Spiritual Enlightenment

Praying 101 for Men

Praying 101 for Women

Praying 101 for Kids & Teens

Praying 101 for Parents

The Feeling

Introduction

I began to think about the word "**Trust**," and wondered do we really know what it means? And do we really **trust**?

I think, like most things in life are, **trust** is something that has been taken for granted. Major assumptions have been implied by it and it is a word that is merely said more than it is experienced.

This book is designed with the intent of calling forth your awareness to **trust** in your life.

Read each question and take a few moments to reflect on what it means to you. Does it apply in your life? Did you automatically think it did, but now that you ask yourself about the different areas in your life, well, maybe just maybe **trust** is not as much a part of your life as you actually thought it was or is.

Trust has been defined as; reliance on the integrity, strength, ability, serenity, etc., of a person or thing; confidence.

Trust has been defined as confident expectation of something; hope.

Trust has been defined as a person whom or thing on which someone relies.

Trust has been defined as the condition of one to whom someone has been entrusted.

Trust has been defined as charge, custody or care.

Trust has been defined as believing; rely or depend on.

If you experience any difficulties answering the questions, change the word "**Trust**" to "Believe".

Do you *really* **trust** that your mother loved you?

Do you *really* **trust** that
the sun will rise
tomorrow?

Do you *really* **trust** that you will always have a roof over your head?

Do you *really* **trust** that you are as smart as you should be right now?

Do you *really* **trust** that God or the Universe or whomever or whatever you believe in, will always provide for you?

Do you *really* **trust** in love?

Do you *really* **trust** that you will never go hungry?

Do you *really* **trust** that somewhere someone loves you?

Do you *really* **trust** that you will always have all the money you need?

Do you *really* **trust** that there is an answer to all your questions?

Do you *really* **trust** that your friends will be there for you as you have been there for them?

Do you *really* **trust** that your friends will tell you the truth about what you are asking, or see your asking as an opportunity to tell you their truth?

Do you *really* **trust** that
if you do a kind deed
for someone you will
be rewarded in other
areas of your life?

Do you *really* **trust** that everything happens the way it is supposed to?

Do you *really* **trust** in signs and signals when something is or isn't working?

Do you *really* **trust** that everything in your life happens for your benefit, for you to grow and learn from?

Do you *really* **trust** that your spouse or significant other loves you?

Do you *really* **trust** that your employer treats you fairly?

Do you *really* **trust** that what you say is in accordance with what you believe?

Do you *really* **trust** that the sun will set tomorrow?

Do you *really* **trust** that you will only cross paths with individuals, both good and bad, who are beneficial for your growth?

Do you *really* **trust** that life is fair?

Do you *really* **trust** that there is more to you than what you wear or own?

Do you *really* **trust** in your level of integrity?

Do you *really* **trust** that you will be safe from a devastating accident?

Do you *really* **trust** that you will be spared from suffering an awful disease?

Do you *really* **trust** that all your needs will be provided for?

Do you *really* **trust** that when meeting someone for the first time that they are meeting the real you, or, a you that they might like better?

Do you *really* **trust** that when flying on a plane, you will have a safe landing?

Do you *really* **trust** that all bad behavior will be punished, one way or another, in this lifetime or another?

Do you *really* **trust** that you know who your father really was or is, or the person he wanted you to *believe* he was or is?

Do you *really* **trust** that there is such a thing as unconditional love?

Do you *really* **trust** that your pets love you unconditionally?

Do you *really* **trust** that
you are capable of
loving
unconditionally?

Do you *really* **trust** that you are capable of being loved unconditionally?

Do you *really* **trust** that someone loves you unconditionally?

Do you *really* **trust** that you know what it means to love unconditionally?

Do you *really* **trust** that your perception is your reality?

Do you *really* **trust** that you are doing the job you are supposed to do?

Do you *really* **trust** that there is goodness in everyone?

Do you *really* **trust** in the concept of sharing?

Do you *really* **trust** in
the value of the truth?

Do you *really* **trust** that you are the best person you can possibly be?

Do you *really* **trust** that you are a fair person?

Do you *really* **trust** in the concept of commitment?

Do you *really* **trust** that people come into your life for a reason or a season?

Do you *really* **trust** that you are polite to everyone that you meet?

Do you *really* **trust** that the relationship you are in is the best one for you?

Do you *really* **trust** that that someone else's perception is their reality?

Do you *really* **trust** that you say what you mean?

Do you *really* **trust** that you mean what you say?

Do you *really* **trust** in what you believe to be your truth?

Do you *really* **trust** that you can identify the truth from a lie?

Do you *really* **trust** that
if you don't lie to
someone, they won't
lie to you?

Do you *really* **trust** in the concept of Heaven and Hell?

Do you *really* **trust** that good will be rewarded and evil will be punished?

Do you *really* **trust** in the evolution of your soul?

Do you *really* **trust** that you are responsible for the life you have chosen to live?

Do you *really* **trust** that your conscious actions are a result of your unconscious actions?

Do you *really* **trust** that your prayers are answered?

Do you *really* **trust** that you are being the best person you can possibly be?

Do you *really* **trust** that everything you see is exactly as you see it?

Do you *really* **trust** that what may appear to be one way, might actually be another?

Do you *really* **trust** that you always have all the information needed to make a decision?

Do you *really* **trust** in everything you hear?

Do you *really* **trust** in everything you see?

Do you *really* **trust** in everything everyone does believing that what they are doing is actually what they intended to do?

Do you *really* **trust** in things that can't be seen?

Do you *really* **trust** in the value you place on your life?

Do you *really* **trust** in the value you have placed on someone else's life?

Do you *really* **trust** in your worthiness?

Do you *really* **trust** in the worthiness of others?

Do you *really* **trust** in the integrity of others?

Do you *really* **trust** in your compassion?

Do you *really* **trust** in the compassion of others?

Do you *really* **trust** in silence?

Do you *really* **trust** in
the silence of others?

Do you *really* **trust** in your actions?

Do you *really* **trust** that your intentions will always be in accordance with your actions?

Do you *really* **trust** that your intentions are in the best interest of all involved?

Do you *really* **trust** that your actions are in the best interest of all involved?

Do you *really* **trust** in
the value of your faith?

Do you *really* **trust** in the value of someone else's faith?

Do you *really* **trust** that
God is where you think
He is?

Do you *really* **trust** that God is doing what He is supposed to be doing?

Do you *really* **trust** that that you possess the power to hurt another individual?

Do you *really* **trust** that you know who you are?

Do you *really* **trust** in
the enthusiasm you
feel in your life?

Do you *really* **trust** that your actions are not those of a hypocrite?

Instructions

Reread this book and look at your answers. For each question ask yourself if the **trust** you believe you have is shown in your actions.

What people say and what they actually do are often totally different. It's the action that speaks volumes. If you say you want to get hit by a big wave, as you stand at the edge of the ocean, and the big wave is upon you and you turn to run, where is the truth? You may have thought it was in your words; however, the reality is in your actions.

What does this mean? Does it mean you lie? Not necessarily. What you say is what you honestly believe about yourself. The action is your true self. What you say is a combination of thoughts and beliefs about yourself that you have accumulated over a lifetime.

The action in the moment is the truth – not the thought and not the reaction.

If you *really* **trust**… then it is not necessary to control a situation with actions.

www.ingramcontent.com/pod-product-compliance
Lightning Source LLC
Chambersburg PA
CBHW022123280326
41933CB00007B/521